Copyright © 2025 Shemmer & Shlyne Group Inc.,
All rights reserved.

No part of this book may be reproduced, transmitted, downloaded, decompiled, reverse engineered, or stored in or introduced into any information storage and retrieval system, in any form without express permission from the author or publisher, except as permitted by U.S. copyright law. For permission, email ckellesai@gmail.com

This book is dedicated to God.

God showed me the life of a seed
and how it relates to me.

If you take care of the seed,
the seed will take care of you.

KELLESIA SHARAY

THE LIFE OF A SEED

Written BY: KELLESIA SHARAY

The determined girl found some amazing friends—marigolds, squash, and pole beans—to plant with the seedlings. They would help defend the garden from the bully bugs and bad weeds.

The seedlings and their new friends worked together to fight off the bully bugs. The girl helped too, by pulling up the weeds.

She also found another friend named Dill, who helped attract even more helpful friends.
They looked different from the others, but they helped protect the garden too.

Kellesia Sharay (Kelley) has overcome a lifetime of challenges. While she has not escaped from her circumstances unscathed. she bears the scars of these experiences as an example to others that your environment and circumstances do not define you and that you are indeed a seed that can emerge from the dirt as a beautiful bloom. ..

Plant Your Own Seed Activity .

Find a small cup, some soil, and a seed (like a bean or sunflower) Plant your seed, just like in the story! Place it near sunlight and give it a little water every day.

Week	Did I Water My Plant? 💧	Did It Get Sunlight? ☀️	Height
1	Yes No	Yes No	
2	Yes No	Yes No	
3	Yes No	Yes No	
4	Yes No	Yes No	

Count the Corn

How many corn ears can you see in this picture?

If I Had a Garden...

What would you plant and why? How would you stop bully bugs? Who would help you care for your garden?

Garden Friends Sorting Game
Take a look at these friends and enemies of the garden, seperate them out!

My Corn
Take a look at these photos of the corn from my own garden

About DeXa Family Gardens

The mission of DeXa Family Gardens, Inc. is to advocate, educate, and empower the community to grow gardens. As we share our knowledge with others, we hope to improve community health, one seed at a time.

Gardening quiets the mind, connects people with the earth, and grounds people within their local neighborhood.

Learn More at

www.dexafamilygardens.org

Feel free to contact us with any questions

info@dexafamilygardens.org

www.ingramcontent.com/pod-product-compliance
Lightning Source LLC
Chambersburg PA
CBHW041403010526
44107CB00015B/1057